For my dearest friend, I wouldn't want to explore creation with anyone else

A Case for a Designer
A Junior Investigator's Guide
Published by In-De and Friends Media, 2025

Text Copyright © 2025 Billie J York
Illustrations Copyright © 2025 Billie J York

Printed in the USA.

All the characters in this book are fictitious, and any resemblance to actual persons living or dead is purely coincidental.

All rights reserved. No part of this publication may be reproduced, distributed, or transmitted in any form or by any means, or stored in a database or retrieval system, without the prior written permission
of the copyright holder.

All inquiries should be directed to
info@in-deandfriends.com

ISBN 979-8-9996401-3-0

A Case for a Designer
A Junior Investigator's Guide

written & illustrated by
Billie J York

In-De and Friends Media

"Hello, my name is Joshua. I love to explore the world and search for patterns that others might miss. Everywhere I look—in the smallest leaf to the widest sky—I see clues that point to something greater. My mission is to follow those clues and reveal the design hidden in the world around us and the sky above.

But I can't do it alone—I'd love for you to come along with me. Together, we'll search, discover, and uncover mysteries that tell a bigger story- patterns of a designer."

"The world is full of truth, waiting for us to see it."

CONTENTS:

Case File 001: Spirals   Page 7

Case File 002: Fractals   Page 19

Case File 003: Hexagons   Page 29

Case File 004: Vibrations Page 39

CASE FILE # 001

SPIRALS

This case takes us deep into the twisty, turning world of spirals- clues hidden in both the tiny and the gigantic.

Evidence

- Milky Way Galaxy
  - Tornado
  - Sea Shell
  - Snail Shell
  - Sunflower
  - Your Inner Ear
    - DNA

Under the cover of night, a swirling band of light stretches across the sky. This is our home galaxy — the Milky Way. From far away, it forms a grand spiral with arms curling gracefully around its center, like a cinnamon roll in space. Billions of stars, clouds of gas, and mysterious dust work together to make a pattern so big, we can't see it all from Earth. But clues from telescopes reveal the twist: the same spiral design we've spotted in seashells and hurricanes is written across the heavens.

 Yummy!!!

A dark cloud twists down from the sky, spinning faster than a race car on a track. This is a tornado — a powerful spiral of wind that can tear up trees, toss cars, and change the land in minutes. At its center is a column of air moving in a tight circle, just like the spirals we've seen in seashells and galaxies. But this spiral is alive with motion, growing and shrinking as it moves across the land. Investigators know: even in the fiercest storms, the pattern remains the same — order hidden inside what seems like chaos.

On the shore, the waves leave behind a trail of clues — seashells of every shape and size. Look closely, and many hide a spiral pattern that winds inward, tighter and tighter, like a staircase built by the sea. Each twist follows a precise mathematical design, the same kind found in sunflowers, galaxies, and storms. These shells aren't built in a hurry; they grow slowly, adding new layers in perfect proportion. For an investigator, every seashell is a case of design hiding in plain sight — a pattern you can hold in your hand.

Our friend In-De, carries his evidence everywhere — a perfect spiral shell on his back. The curve starts small at the center and widens with every turn, following the same precise pattern we've spotted in galaxies,

storms, and seashells. In-De doesn't measure or draw his spiral; it grows naturally, layer by layer, as he gets older. His shell is more than a home — it's living proof that the spiral design is built right into creation.

In the middle of a sunflower's bright face is a secret design — hundreds of tiny seeds arranged in two sets of spirals, curving in opposite directions. No ruler, no blueprint, yet each seed fits perfectly without wasting space. This pattern follows a special number sequence that shows up in pine cones, shells, and even hurricanes. Investigators know this isn't just pretty — it's efficient, natural engineering at its finest, written in the language of spirals.

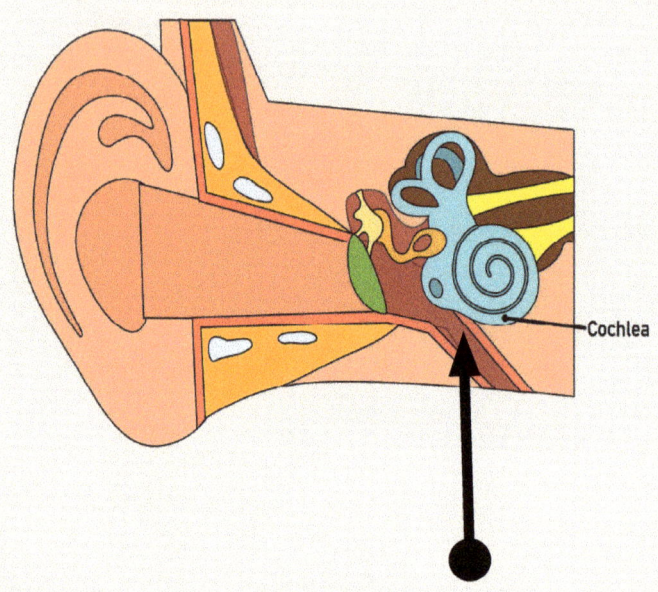

Let's go a little bit smaller, and look inside ourselves. Deep inside your ear is a hidden spiral – the cochlea. It's curled up like a tiny snail shell, smaller than your fingernail, but packed with incredible design. Inside, fluid moves when sound enters your ear, and thousands of tiny hair-like sensors turn those movements into messages your brain can understand. Without this spiral, music, laughter, and the sound of crashing waves would be nothing but silence. Even in the secret chambers of our own bodies, the spiral shows up – a pattern of purpose we carry everywhere we go.

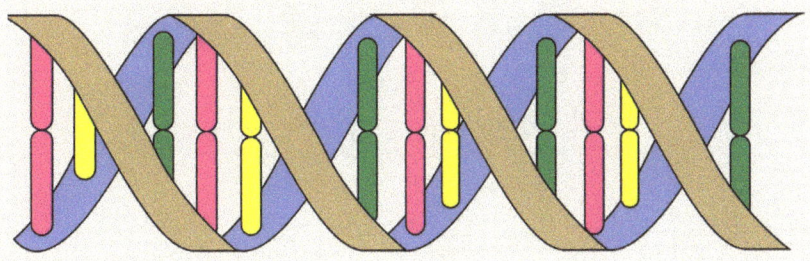

At the smallest scale of all, a spiral holds the master plan for every living thing — DNA. It's a twisted ladder called a double helix, so small you'd need a powerful microscope to see it. Each rung of the ladder is made of a special chemical code that tells cells how to build and repair a living body — whether it's a whale, a sunflower, or you. The design is so precise, even the tiniest change can make a huge difference. From galaxies swirling in space to the spiral tucked inside your very cells, the pattern is everywhere. For this investigator, the evidence is clear: spirals aren't an accident — they're a signature. But a signature of who?

CASE CLOSED:

Pattern Detected

From the roar of a tornado, to the quiet curve of a snail's shell, from the blazing arms of the Milky Way, to the tiny twist of DNA inside our cells- the spiral shows up again and again. Big or small, slow or fast, each spiral follows a path of precision, beauty, and purpose. As investigators, we've tracked the clues across land, sea, sky, and even within ourselves.

The evidence is stacked, the pattern undeniable. The spiral isn't random — it's a master design, we see throughout the world, the sky above and inside us.

Just like your grandma made the cinnamon roll, someone had to have made the spiral.

Activity At Home:

Become a spiral detective! Search your house, yard, or neighborhood for real-life spirals. Document your work on the pages provided.

Your Mission:

Search for spirals where you live and record your clues!

Steps:

1. Look Around – Check your kitchen, yard, or neighborhood for spiral shapes (shells, pinecones, flower centers, swirls in food, cords, etc.).

2. Record Evidence – Draw the spiral or take a photo. Write down where you found it.

3. Report Back – Share your findings with family or friends. See if they can find more spirals!

Investigator's Tip:

Some spirals hide in plain sight. Look closely and from different angles!

Investigator's Notepaper

CASE FILE # 002

FRACTALS

From the flash of lightning to the veins in leaves, trees, lungs, and even snowflakes, nature loves a pattern that repeats itself. We call these fascinating designs fractals!

Evidence

- Lightning
  - Trees
  - Leaves
  - Lungs
- Snowflakes

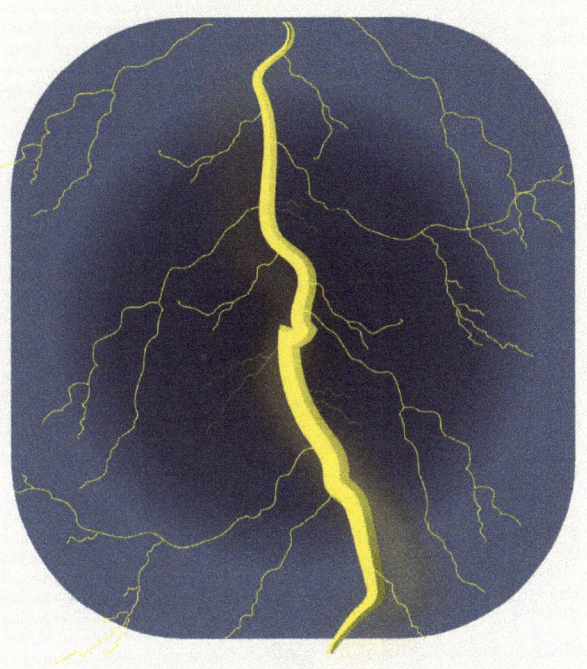

Crack! Boom! A bolt of lightning splits the sky, branching in every direction. Each main branch divides into smaller branches, and those divide again—just like the twigs of a tree.

This repeating, branching pattern is a perfect example of a fractal. Whether it's a quick flash in a summer storm or a powerful strike during a blizzard, lightning shows us how nature loves to repeat its designs, even in the blink of an eye.

From the sturdy trunk, to the tiniest twigs, a tree's branches follow a repeating pattern. The main trunk splits into large branches, those branches split into smaller ones, and those split again—over and over—just like the forks of lightning. This repeating design helps the tree reach sunlight from every direction, and it's a perfect example of how nature uses fractals to grow strong and beautiful.

Look closely at a leaf—whether it's bright green, sunny yellow, warm orange, or deep red—you'll see

tiny lines called veins. One big vein runs down the middle, smaller ones branch off, and those split again into even tinier lines—just like branches on a tree. This fractal pattern helps carry water and food to every part of the leaf, like little highways, so the whole leaf can stay healthy and full of color.

Sidenote: Did you also know trees and leaves make oxygen you breathe?

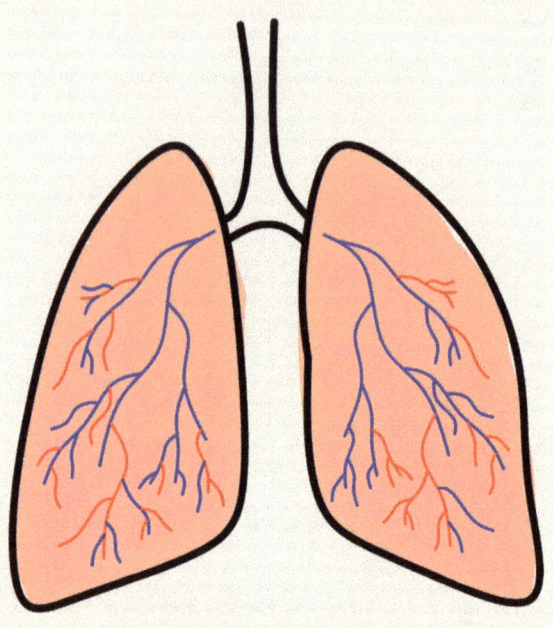

Inside your chest are two amazing organs—your lungs! Their main airways split into smaller tubes, and those split again and again, just like the branches of a tree.

This fractal pattern is super important because it helps spread air to millions of tiny air sacs, called alveoli. That's where oxygen from the air gets into your blood, and carbon dioxide leaves your body. Without this branching design, your lungs couldn't reach every tiny corner, and your body wouldn't get the fresh air it needs to keep you running, playing, and growing strong.

Every snowflake starts as a tiny ice crystal high in the clouds. As it falls through cold, moist air, it begins to grow arms that branch out, and those branches grow even smaller branches—just like a fractal! The colder the air and the longer the journey, the more branches form. The amazing thing is, each snowflake follows the same repeating pattern, but no two are exactly alike. This fractal design helps the snowflake grow quickly and beautifully, turning a winter storm into millions of tiny, frozen works of art. Next time snow falls, remember—you're seeing a sky full of nature's perfect little patterns.

CASE CLOSED:

Pattern Detected

From lightning bolts to leafy veins, from the branches of trees to the airways in our lungs, and even the icy arms of snowflakes—fractals are everywhere! They are patterns that repeat, smaller and smaller, helping nature build, grow, and work in the smartest ways possible. Whether they carry air, water, or energy, fractals make sure nothing is wasted. Once you know what to look for, you'll start spotting these amazing designs all around you. Look closely at winding rivers seen from above, the shape of a coastline, coral in the ocean, or even broccoli on your plate—you might be surprised at what counts as a fractal! Keep your eyes open, detective.

Did someone use the same brushstroke across the whole world, even inside us?

Activity At Home:

Alright, junior detectives—grab your magnifying glass and your notepaper! Your mission is to search for fractal patterns hiding in your world, from the veins in a leaf to the branches of a puddle after it rains.

Search for fractals where you live and record your clues!

Steps:

1. Leaf Investigation

Find a leaf and look at how the veins branch out. Draw what you see.

2. Tree or Plant Sketch

Look at a tree or plant and sketch how the branches split into smaller branches.

3. Broccoli Break

Look closely at broccoli or cauliflower and notice how each floret looks like a tiny version of the whole.

Investigator Tip:
Hold your hand up to the light and look closely at the veins under your skin. See how a big vein branches into smaller ones, and those branch again? That's another fractal pattern, inside you!

Investigator's Notepaper

CASE FILE # 003

HEXAGONS

A six-sided mystery appears often in nature. Strong, efficient, and beautiful, the hexagon is a master of design.

Evidence

- Bees: Honeycombs
- Wasps: Nest
- Turtle: Shells
- Insects: Eyes
- The Secret Hexagon in You

A beehive is a masterpiece of design. Each wax cell is shaped like a perfect hexagon, fitting together with no gaps and wasting no space. This six-sided pattern makes the walls strong enough to hold golden honey and protect growing bees. Without ever learning geometry, bees instinctively know to build in this shape — a pattern written into their very nature. The honeycomb is more than a home for bees; it is a food source for countless creatures, including people. The beeswax is used for candles, polish, and even medicines, while the honey inside stores the sun's energy for months. Without healthy honeycombs, bees could not thrive — and without bees, much of our world's plants and crops would not grow.

The wasp nest may look like a villain's lair, and its residents may seem like troublemakers, but its shape is nothing short of brilliant. Built from chewed wood fibers mixed with saliva, the walls form a cluster of perfect hexagons — each one a sturdy nursery for growing wasps. This design is strong, light, and efficient, holding together with the strength of nature's geometry. Layer upon layer of paper-like walls protect the colony inside, keeping the young safe until they are ready to fly. Even the wasps, though fierce, have their role in the grand scheme of things — controlling pests, and pollinating plants, helps keep the balance in the natural world. Without them, many insect populations would grow out of control, upsetting the delicate order of life.

Shelby the turtle loves to jump off rocks. Can you see his shell? Here is a close-up.

The top, called the carapace, is covered with strong plates arranged in a perfect pattern of hexagons. These six-sided shapes fit together like puzzle pieces, creating sturdy armor that protects Shelby from harm. Each hexagon is part of a living structure, connected to his bones and growing with him over time. His shell is more than protection — it's also his home, giving him a safe place to retreat whenever danger is near. Strong, light, and built to last, this design helps Shelby and other turtles survive and thrive in the grand design of life.

Have you ever wondered why it's so hard to catch a fly? Take a closer look — even closer — and you'll discover that many insect eyes are covered in tiny repeating hexagons. These are the lenses of a compound eye, called ommatidia, and most insects have them: bees, wasps, dragonflies, flies, and even butterflies. The hexagon shape is nature's perfect way to pack thousands of lenses tightly together with no gaps, wrapping them over a curved surface. This design gives insects a wide field of view and helps them detect the slightest movement. Those thousands of hexagon lenses allow them to see in almost every direction at once, making it nearly impossible to sneak up on them. Even the quickest motion is spotted right away, giving the insect time to dart, hop, or take flight. From the air, on the ground, or among flowers, these hexagon-packed eyes help insects survive.

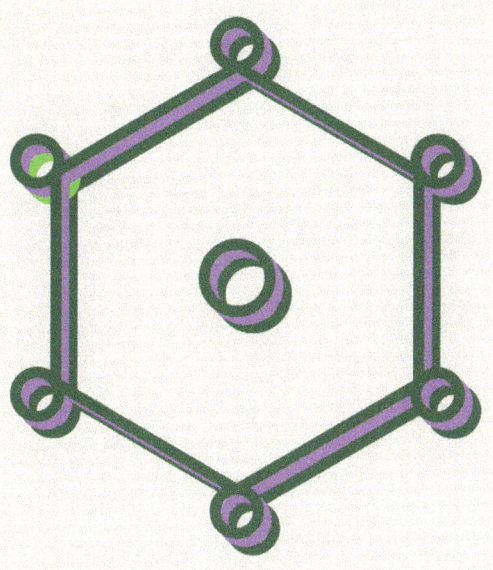

You might think hexagons only belong to bees, turtles, and dragonflies — but there's a secret: they're inside you too! Not as little shapes you can see, but as part of the molecules that make your body work.

Deep inside your cells, some of the building blocks of life are made from six carbon atoms locked together in a hexagon. Scientists call this shape a benzene ring. You can find it in parts of your DNA (the "recipe" for you), in some of the proteins that build your muscles, and even in certain vitamins that keep you healthy. This hidden hexagon is one of nature's favorite tools for making strong, stable molecules. Without it, life as we know it would not work the same way.

So the next time you see a honeycomb, remember — that amazing hexagon design is part of the grand plan of life- and it's hiding in you, too!

CASE CLOSED:
Pattern Detected

From the buzzing hive to the deep blue sea, the hexagon proves itself as one of nature's smartest designs. Bees build honeycombs from perfect hexagons to store honey and protect their young. Wasps, though fierce, shape their papery nests from the same pattern, creating strong, light nurseries. On land, turtles carry a shield of hexagons on their backs, each plate locking with the next for strength and safety. Insects use them too — the hexagon forms the surface of compound eyes, letting creatures like dragonflies and flies see nearly all around them at once.

Humans have borrowed this brilliant shape for our own engineering — from honeycomb cores in airplane wings to lightweight building materials and space-saving tiles. Even inside you, the benzene ring — a tiny carbon hexagon — is part of the molecules that make life possible.

You have to wonder, who decided the hexagon, with its strength and elegance would make a wonderful pattern of design?

Activity At Home:

Mission Brief: Your next case is to spot and create hexagons! Use these activities to see how this six-sided shape shows up in amazing ways.

Build-a-Bee Cell

Use craft sticks, drinking straws, or rolled paper to make one hexagon. See how many you can fit together without leaving gaps.

Turtle Shell Art

Draw the outline of a turtle shell, then fill it in with hexagons. Color each hexagon a different shade to make your own turtle pattern.

Insect Eye Zoom-In

Use bubble wrap as a pretend "insect eye." Hold it over a picture in a magazine or book and notice how it breaks the image into tiny shapes.

Investigator Tip:

Six sides are stronger than you think — that's why nature uses them for armor, storage, and even super sight!

Investigator's Notepaper

> **CASE FILE #004**

VIBRATIONS

You can't always see them, but you can hear and feel them. The hidden pattern of vibrations is all around you — in the air, in water, and even in the ground beneath your feet.

Evidence

- Human sound waves
- Bio-sonar and Echolocation
- Heartbeat EKG
- Cymatics
- Earth's Hum

"Do you see these waves? They're coming from me! When I talk—or even sing—my voice shakes the air. That shaking makes sound waves, and those waves carry my voice to your ears. The musical notes floating around me are just a picture of what's really happening all the time. Every sound, from the strum of a guitar to the honk of a goose, begins with vibrations. The faster the air vibrates, the higher the sound, like a whistle. The slower it vibrates, the lower the sound, like a drum. So right now, as I sing, I'm sending invisible waves racing through the air. Want to prove it? Place your hand gently on your throat while you hum—you can actually feel the vibrations buzzing inside of you!"

"Remember in Case File 001, that tiny spiral in your ear? The cochlea? That is how you hear me, it feels the vibrations."

Dolphins and bats both use an incredible skill called echolocation, also known as biosonar. Instead of relying only on sight, they send out high-pitched sound vibrations into their surroundings. When those vibrations hit an object, they bounce back as echoes. By listening carefully to the echoes, the animal can figure out the size, shape, distance, and even movement of what's around them.

For dolphins, echolocation makes it possible to hunt for fish in dark, cloudy water. For bats, it means they can fly swiftly through the night, dodging trees and catching tiny insects in midair. Their brains turn these returning vibrations into a kind of "sound picture," letting them see with sound.

Your heart is more than a pump—it's a powerful source of vibrations. With every beat, the heart's muscles contract and push blood through the body. That pumping creates vibrations that ripple through your chest and keep a steady rhythm of life. Doctors use stethoscopes to listen to those vibrations, turning them into the familiar lub-dub sound of a heartbeat.

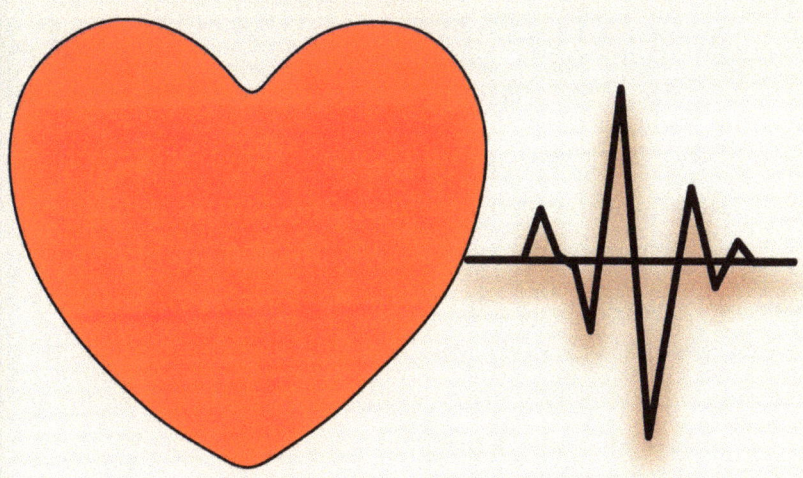

These vibrations are important clues about our health. A steady rhythm shows the heart is working well, while an uneven beat can signal something's wrong. Just like sound waves in music, the heart's vibrations follow a pattern—a design that keeps your whole body alive and in motion.

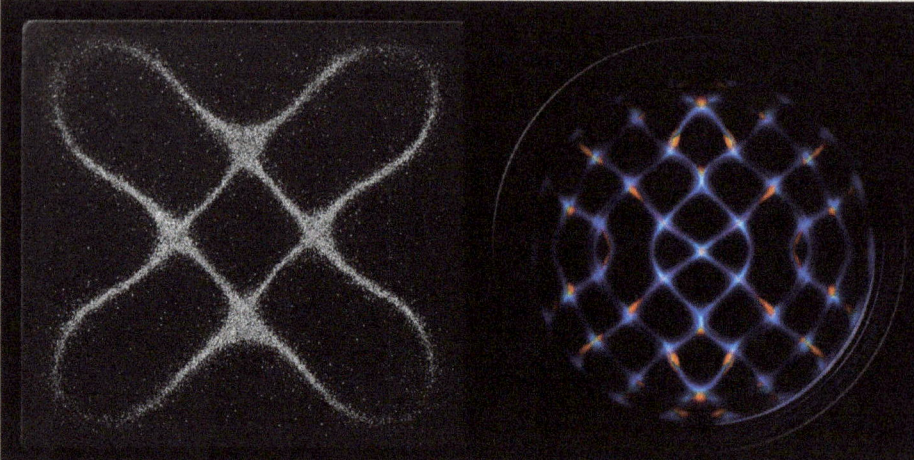

Cymatics is the science of seeing sound. When vibrations move through different materials, they create hidden patterns that suddenly become visible. On a Chladni plate, sand scatters into geometric designs as the metal vibrates at certain frequencies. The lines where the sand gathers are places with no movement—called nodal lines.

Water reveals the same mystery in a different way. When sound waves pass through it, ripples form into dazzling, flower-like shapes that change with the pitch. Higher frequencies make more complex patterns, while lower ones stay simpler.

Both the plate and the water prove something amazing: vibrations aren't random. They follow order and design, leaving behind patterns we can see with our eyes— shapes born from sound itself.

Did you know the Earth has its very own song? Scientists call it the "Earth's hum," and it's a constant vibration that never stops. Even when everything around you feels quiet, the planet beneath your feet is gently shaking with low, deep sound waves. They're so soft and slow that our ears can't hear them—but special instruments can record them.

This hum is created by natural forces: ocean waves rolling across the seafloor, winds rushing through the atmosphere, and even earthquakes sending energy through the ground. Together, they keep the Earth vibrating like a giant musical instrument.

Most people don't realize our planet is always singing. But once you know, it changes the way you think about silence. Beneath every step you take, the Earth is alive with hidden music—a rhythm that's been playing since the very beginning.

CASE CLOSED:
Pattern Detected

Everywhere we investigated, vibrations pointed to order, not chaos. Joshua's voice, the dolphin's and bat's echolocation, the steady heartbeat, even the Earth's quiet hum—all of them show that vibrations aren't accidents or leftovers. Vibrations are patterns—structured, repeatable, and purposeful—woven into the world by a grand design.

They move through air, water, and solid ground with rules that can be tested and trusted. When we measure them, we find rhythm. When we watch them, we see structure. When we listen, we hear meaning.

Maybe the Designer made vibrations part of life's foundation so we could see how everything is held together in rhythm.

Activity At Home:

Get ready, Junior Investigator—now it's your turn to experiment and uncover the hidden patterns of vibrations right at home!

1. The Rice Drum Test

Stretch plastic wrap tightly over the top of a bowl and secure it with a rubber band. Sprinkle a few grains of rice on top. Now tap the side of the bowl or clap nearby—watch as the rice jumps and dances from the vibrations moving through the air!

2. Hum a Song

Place your fingers gently on your throat and hum a tune. You'll feel the buzzing vibrations as your voice shakes the air. Try singing higher and lower notes—notice how the vibrations change with pitch.

3. Feel Your Heartbeat

Sit quietly for a moment, then place your hand over your chest or on the side of your neck where your pulse beats. Every thump you feel is a vibration—your heart sending waves of life through your whole body.

Investigator Tip: Vibrations are everywhere—listen, feel, and watch closely,

Investigator's Notepaper

CONCLUSION:

Our investigation is complete. From spirals tucked into shells and galaxies, to fractals branching through trees and lightning, to hexagons hidden in hives and turtle shells, and even the secret hum of the Earth—every case pointed to the same truth. Patterns are everywhere. They are not random, they are not accidents. They are the fingerprints of a grand design woven into creation itself.

As junior investigators, we set out to uncover mysteries. What we discovered is that the world is filled with order, beauty, and meaning—written into the very structure of nature. Even the vibrations that carry sound and heartbeat reveal that life itself is full of rhythm and harmony.

And these are only a few examples—keep your eyes open, because patterns can be found everywhere, waiting to be discovered.

The universe is filled with shapes born from sound itself—designs spoken into motion by an Intelligent Designer.

Books available from In-De and Friends Media

Patterns by Design: A Little Snail Explores Creation
ISBN: 979-8-9996401-0-9
Paperback

Patterns by Design: A Little Snail Explores Creation
ISBN: 979-8-9996401-1-6
Hardback

Patterns by Design Activity Book
ISBN: 979-8-9996401-2-3
Paperback

www.ingramcontent.com/pod-product-compliance
Lightning Source LLC
Chambersburg PA
CBHW052034030426
42337CB00027B/5001